CONTENTS

Front endpapers:
Pterois volitans and *Chaetodon xanthocephalus.* Photo by D. Terver, Nancy Aquarium, France.

Frontis:
Platax pinnatus subadult. Photo by Miloslav Kocar.

Back endpapers:
Glyphidodontops hemicyaneus. Photo by Dr. Gerald R. Allen.

© 1979 by T.F.H. Publications, Inc. Ltd.

KW-031

ISBN 0-87666-513-X

Distributed in the UNITED STATES by T.F.H. Publications, Inc., 211 West Sylvania Avenue, Neptune City, NJ 07753; in CANADA by H & L Pet Supplies Inc., 27 Kingston Crescent, Kitchener, Ontario N2B 2T6; Rolf C. Hagen Ltd., 3225 Sartelon Street, Montreal 382 Quebec; in ENGLAND by T.F.H. (Great Britain) Ltd., 11 Ormside Way, Holmethorpe Industrial Estate, Redhill, Surrey RH1 2PX; in AUSTRALIA AND THE SOUTH PACIFIC by T.F.H. (Australia) Pty. Ltd., Box 149, Brookvale 2100 N.S.W., Australia; in NEW ZEALAND by Ross Haines & Son, Ltd., 18 Monmouth Street, Grey Lynn, Auckland 2 New Zealand; in SINGAPORE AND MALAYSIA by MPH Distributors Pte., 71-77 Stamford Road, Singapore 0617; in the PHILIPPINES by Bio-Research, 5 Lippay Street, San Lorenzo Village, Makati, Rizal; in SOUTH AFRICA by Multipet Pty. Ltd., 30 Turners Avenue, Durban 4001. Published by T.F.H. Publications Inc., Ltd., the British Crown Colony of Hong Kong. THIS IS THE 1983 EDITION.

MARINE FISH

by DR. HERBERT R. AXELROD
and
DR. WARREN E. BURGESS

Pygoplites diacanthus, a brightly colored angelfish suitable for home aquaria. Photo by H. Debelius. Below: *Coris aygula*, a colorful wrasse. The juvenile (shown here) can dive into the sand when frightened.

Introduction

The successful keeping of the brilliantly colored coral reef fishes is now well within the capacity of most advanced aquarists and even many beginners. Gone are the days when a marine aquarist was a special breed who by costly trial and error or by just plain luck was able to maintain these fishes for a reasonable length of time. Today there are a large number of marine aquarists who, by virtue of the knowledge passed on by earlier aquarists and new equipment that overcomes many of the earlier problems, are able to keep these fishes for such a long time that they either outgrow the tanks or die of old age. The marine aquarium has reached a stage where it can now successfully compete with its freshwater counterpart.

Coupled with these technological advances in the actual keeping of the fishes is the increased knowledge of the fishes themselves. Their daily habits, feeding preferences (or needs), compatible tankmates, and even breeding behavior are more completely known and the previous mistakes, often leading to the demise of many fishes, are made less and less often.

As the demand for marine fishes grows, the shipping techniques become more refined so that many more fishes, even from the other side of the world, make the journey more safely and in better health. This has helped reduce their cost so that some of the more common and hardy marine fishes can compete in price with freshwater fishes. It also means that instead of relying solely on fishes that come from relatively short distances (Florida, etc.), the marine hobbyist can expect to be able to keep fishes from places like Sri Lanka, Africa, the Red Sea, Australia, and the Philippines. Even our Hawaiian fishes make the journey more safely.

It must be remembered, however, that there are certain rules that must be followed. Anyone who wants to maintain marine fishes must learn these rules, even if he was an expert in the keeping of freshwater fishes. Although some of the procedures are similar, others are radically different. It may even be of some advantage for a novice to try marine fishes without any previous experience in fishkeeping at all. Then there would be no tendency to apply freshwater practices to the marine tank.

Even though marine aquaria are a little more complicated than freshwater aquaria, the techniques are easy to learn, and the novice soon becomes an expert in the field. It is well worth this little extra effort to be able to keep the colorful reef fishes.

THE TANK

Undoubtedly, one of the most important advances in

aquarium technology in recent years that has caused marine aquarium keeping to become much safer for the fishes has been the development of the all-glass tank. Almost every book or article written for the beginning aquarist has stated in bold letters: do not let any metal surface come in contact with the water in your marine tank. Good advice certainly, but what was the aquarist to do when the only available aquaria were built of stainless steel and glass? Many remedies were tried with varying success to prevent this contact (usually by covering the metal surfaces and seams with a variety of different substances), but most of the remedies did not work, did not work for long, or even contributed to the early demise of the fishes. Although the marine aquarist still has to keep a sharp eye out for metal contact, the basic piece of starting equipment, the tank, is now safe. Fortunately, all-glass tanks are readily available in an array of sizes and priced so low as to be even less expensive than the older stainless steel tanks.

Get the largest tank possible. Although certain species (seahorses, etc.) can be kept in relatively small aquaria, any marine aquarium of less than 25 gallons capacity is difficult to maintain. If anything goes wrong the smaller tanks get wiped out very quickly, for they do not have the volume to combat sudden changes or even a small influx of pollutants. The larger tanks also allow the aquarist to get more of a variety of fishes and to allow room for their growth.

It is advisable to provide a cover for the tank in order to keep evaporation at a low level and the fishes in the tank. Remember that the supports for the cover should be of a material other than metal that will not release toxic substances when it comes in contact with the salt water.

OTHER EQUIPMENT

The pump can be selected on the same basis as that for a freshwater tank. It must have the capacity to easily handle the aeration and filtration systems for the size tank that has

1

2

3

10

4

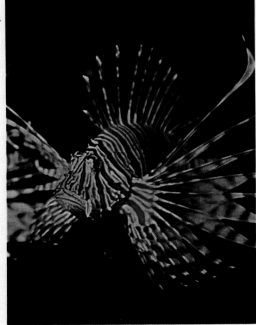

1. *Hippocampus erectus* male giving birth. 2. *Hippocampus erectus* male holding on to a marine plant. 3. *Hippocampus kuda* individuals holding on to each other. 4. *Pterois lunulata* stalking its prey. 5. *Pterois volitans* among the coral of an aquarium. (Photos 1, 2. Wm.Stephens. 3. CLI. 4. Dr. Herbert R. Axelrod. 5. Dr. D. Terver, Nancy Aquarium).

5

been selected. Perhaps at the start an extra airstone or two can be used with the idea that if more power is needed for filtration these can be shut down and the air diverted to an extra filter. Power filters, in which the pump is an actual part of the filter, are often utilized in marine tanks with very good results. These have the disadvantages, however, of (1) placing a metal object in proximity to the water of the tank and (2) the pump itself can be damaged by the salt from the aquarium.

The heater must be able to properly heat the tank to a temperature of 70°-85°F (21°-30°C). Most heaters will have instructions on the box as to what size tank they are designed for, and a dealer's advice is usually available. In large tanks it may be advisable to use two heaters, one on either end. This enables the tank to heat up more uniformly, and if one heater fails, the other will maintain a suitable temperature until the first can be replaced. Of course with two heaters there will be twice as much risk of heater failure. With larger tanks the "cooling off to dangerous levels" period is much longer than that for smaller tanks which would cool quickly, thus endangering the health of the fishes.

Heaters should be provided with thermostats to keep the temperature within certain limits, and a thermometer must be available to make sure that these limits are not exceeded. Unfortunately, thermostats do break down, so it is necessary to check them often. Any sign of a sudden rise or fall in temperature could spell trouble, and the heaters and thermostats should be checked to see if they are operating properly.

Lights are often used to show off the fishes to their best advantage and to help promote the growth of algae that a number of fishes browse on. Here again the metal of the light and electrical connections are potential troublemakers and can best be separated from the salt water of the tank by a glass cover. Be sure that the glass will be able to support the weight of the fixture and will not crack from the heat of the bulbs. For this reason the cooler fluorescent lights are more popular than the incandescent variety in spite of the higher initial cost. Actually, they are more economical to run, so the cost differential is made up over the long run. In addition there are a variety of fluorescent bulbs which give off light from different points of the spectrum. The "white" or "warm white" bulbs are good for growing algae and at the same time give off a suitable light for viewing the fishes. Special bulbs are designed to promote plant growth and give off a more reddish or violet light. This light enhances the brilliance of many of the fishes which have iridescent colors.

For viewing the fishes, the light is best placed near the front of the tank. Unfortunately this promotes heaviest growth of algae on the front glass, which is generally undesirable. Perhaps it is best to have the light near the back of the tank for algal growth there but moved forward when viewing the fishes.

Always check the electrical connections to see that the salt water hasn't worked its way to them, causing the possibility of shock, either to the fishes or the aquarist himself.

Of prime importance are the filters. There are a variety of filters on the market, many with different purposes. Several of these are useful in marine aquaria in order to (1) remove the larger particles, (2) remove the more minute particles, or (3) remove the unwanted chemicals and gases.

The removal of large particulate matter such as uneaten food, feces, or other polluting substances can be accomplished by the standard outside filter (many different kinds available) in which the water containing the material to be filtered is passed through a layer of polyester wool or other similar substance that allows the water to pass but not the polluting particles. When the filtering medium becomes clogged it can be removed from the filter box,

1. *Paraglyphidodon bonang* juvenile. 2. *Pomacentrus* sp. (probably *P. coelestis*). 3. *Dascyllus trimaculatus* juveniles seeking refuge in an anemone. 4. *Dascyllus aruanus,* an excellent beginner's fish. (Photos 1. Dr. G. R. Allen. 2. Aaron Norman. 3. & 4. Dr. Fujio Yasuda.)

3

4

15

cleaned and replaced.

The diatom filter is designed to filter out very small particles that cloud up an aquarium. The filter medium, finely packed diatom shells, is said to be able to remove material down to the size of bacteria. This helps keep the water crystal-clear but the filter clogs up very quickly. Since it should not be kept on for extended periods of time, the diatom filter can be easily cleaned when not in use.

Synthetic ion exchange resins are used in marine aquaria to absorb some of the heavy metals such as copper. This can be especially useful after the tank has been treated with a copper solution to rid it of certain diseases or pests. Unfortunately, the ion exchange resins are not selective as far as good metals and bad metals are concerned and will remove some of the necessary trace elements along with the unwanted substances. Until more is known about the exact chemistry of the exchange it might be best to forego their use.

Biological filtration is perhaps one of the most important discoveries enabling marine aquarium keeping to be practiced by beginners. The system employs aerobic bacteria to break down the waste products which so frequently foul a tank. These bacteria build up in filter boxes or other areas where wastes accumulate to a point where the waste material created by the fishes is rapidly broken down to harmless substances. When the filter material is replaced or cleaned the bacterial population drops sharply but soon gets back to full strength if enough are left in the tank as "seed." As a matter of fact, new tanks are "inoculated" with some of these bacteria to make sure that their population is large enough to do the work when the fishes are added. Dealers generally will supply the new aquarist with water from an old tank which contains enough of the bacteria to get a culture going in the new tank.

Undergravel filters operate on this principle. The bacterial culture resides among the grains of sand and, as the flow of water carries waste material into the sand where it is trapped, they go to work on it. The flow of water must be sufficient to carry oxygen to the lower levels of the sand, for it is needed by the bacteria to survive. If the oxygen level drops too low the beneficial aerobic bacteria are replaced by anaerobic bacteria, leading to black sand giving off the characteristic "rotten egg smell" of H_2S (hydrogen sulphide). The best material for covering the surface of the subsand filter is crushed shells (shell grit), dolomite, or crushed coral. This material helps the water keep its pH value near the proper levels and, if not used in a subsand filter, should be placed in the outside filter.

Protein skimmers, ozonizers, and ultra-violet light filters seem to be in disfavor in home aquaria these days and are not recommended unless special conditions call for their use.

THE WATER

When marine fishkeeping was starting out, the best medium in which to keep the fishes was sea water collected from an area as free from pollution as possible. Although natural sea water was risky due to its unknown composition, constant changes due to the plankton it contained, and possible disease organisms or parasites that were brought in with it, it was still safer than the early artificial salt mixtures that contained most of the basic ingredients but lacked certain of the trace elements so important to the well-being of the fishes. Two things have reversed this trend: (1) pollution has become so extensive that it is very difficult to find water clean and safe enough for a home aquarium; and (2) the artificial salts have become more and more perfected so that they are reliable enough for keeping even the more delicate species of marine fishes.

As the marine tank ages, certain trace elements are "used up" by the inhabitants and must be replaced. This can be accomplished by adding trace element tablets that are

1
2

3

4

1. *Amphiprion bicinctus* juvenile above anemone. 2. *Amphiprion frenatus* pair guarding eggs in an aquarium. *3. Amphiprion perideraion*, one of the skunk clowns. 4. *Amphiprion ocellaris*, perhaps the most popular aquarium clownfish. (Photos 1. Helmut Debelius. 2. Dr. Herbert R. Axelrod. 3. M. Goto. 4. CLI.)

available commercially or by changing a portion of the old water with new water as is done in many freshwater aquaria. This replacement of the water seems to rejuvenate the tank and keeps it going for longer periods of time than can be expected with tanks in which part of the water is not changed.

To keep tabs on the quality of the water in a marine tank, certain measurements can be made. The specific gravity, or the amount of total dissolved salts in the water, is measured by means of a hydrometer. This instrument, almost certainly available in any marine fish store, is calibrated over a range of from 1.000 to 1.050, with the normal range (around 1.025 at 60°F) usually marked off for easy reference. Since marine aquariums are kept at temperatures above 60°, there is usually a conversion table that goes along with the hydrometer for converting the observed reading to the true value. Roughly, a reading of 1.025 at 60° is equal to 1.023 at 80°. If the specific gravity is too high or too low, the addition of fresh water to reduce it or more concentrated salt water to increase it is easily accomplished.

The pH should be closely watched along with the density. pH is the measurement of the hydrogen ion concentration or, more simply, the acidity or alkalinity of the water. The pH scale runs from 1 to 14, with 7.0 being neutral. Values below 7.0 are considered to be acid, values above it are alkaline. Sea water is alkaline, with a normal pH of 8.2, the aquarium water also being kept at or near this level. If the pH shifts toward the acid side—some drop is acceptable, being normal with living animals in the tank—it should be closely watched to see that it does not drop too far. If the pH drop persists, for example below 7.4, the cause must be discovered and corrected. Kits with the chemicals necessary for adjusting the pH of sea water are available commercially.

One of the major causes of a pH drop is an increase in the

amount of CO_2 accumulated in the tank water. Temporary removal of this gas can be accomplished by increased aeration. However, the cause for the buildup of CO_2 (and the resultant drop in pH) must be corrected immediately. Too many fishes, decaying uneaten food, unremoved feces or an undiscovered dead fish may contribute to or cause the problem. Once the offending material is removed, part of the water must be changed and the aeration increased to bring the chemical balance back to normal.

Nitrites, nitrates, and ammonia should be closely monitored in a marine aquarium. In a newly set-up tank the nitrite and ammonia levels rapidly increase to very high levels and then drop off to a low (safe) level in a few days to a week or so. Once this drop has occurred it is safe to add the fishes. The bacteria have grown in number so that they are able to convert the nitrites to harmless nitrates. Again, there are kits available which enable the aquarist to measure the amounts of ammonia, nitrites, and nitrates in the aquarium. Nitrates, the least harmful of the three, can be tolerated to levels of about 40ppm. Ammonia and nitrites are both very toxic and their levels should be kept as close to zero as practical, although it is said that most fishes can withstand concentrations of as much as 0.1ppm of ammonia and 0.25ppm of nitrites.

DECORATIONS

One of the greatest differences between marine and freshwater aquaria is the type of decorations available. Freshwater aquaria, with the exception of certain cichlid tanks, etc., almost always have a luxuriant growth of plants. Aside from the algae encouraged to grow on the sides of the tank for food, the marine aquarium is almost always devoid of plants. A few daring marine aquarists have been trying to culture some of the marine algae (*Caulerpa,* etc.) but without very much success. For those marine aquarists who must have plants in their aquarium, there are a number of

1

1. *Monacanthus ciliatus* in a defensive posture. 2. *Balistoides conspicillum,* the famous clown trigger. 3. *Lactophys triqueter* from Puerto Rico. 4. A juvenile cowfish, *Lactophrys* sp. 5. A juvenile trunkfish, *Ostracion cubicus.* (Photos 1. CLI. 2. Dr. D. Terver, Nancy Aquarium. 3. Dr. G. R. Allen. 4. Charles Arneson. 5. Dr. Fujio Yasuda.)

2

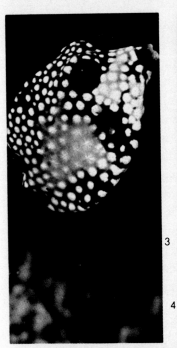

3

4

5

plastic replicas of marine species available that are very realistic and do much to enhance the beauty of the tank.

The basic item for the decoration of marine aquaria is coral. Not living coral, although marine aquarists have tried to keep several species of coral alive in their tanks with varying amounts of success, but the cleaned skeleton. This decorative coral is cleaned very carefully, bleached, and cleaned again until no impurities or dead organisms remain to foul the tank. Before purchasing a piece of coral it is wise to inspect it carefully, making sure there are no overlooked small boring animals that have made it through the cleaning process. Sometimes a slightly foul odor will tip off the aquarist that the coral has not been cleaned thoroughly enough, although by the time the coral reaches the retail store most of the smell would have dissipated. Chances are, however, that the coral for sale at a marine aquarium store for use in a marine aquarium is safe. Safer, less expensive plastic coral is now available and is rapidly replacing the real coral in marine aquaria.

The coral can be placed in the tank just before the water is added. This avoids any miscalculation as to how much water the coral will displace and prevents overflowing. Any suitable arrangement should be okay as long as care is taken that there will be few, if any, areas in which uneaten food, dead fishes, etc. can remain hidden. Certain corals, such as the organ-pipe coral, which have such areas should be taken out and cleaned frequently.

Most other "natural" objects, such as dried sea fans or dried sponges, should be avoided. Again, plastic imitation sea fans and other similar items are sold for the marine aquarium. These are much safer than the real thing.

MARINE SYSTEMS

The currently popular system for maintaining marine aquaria is the biological filtration system. This is the one in which a population of bacteria is encouraged to grow in the filtration system, where they proceed to break down the wastes into less harmful material. The newly set-up tank is inoculated with water containing a seed population of these bacteria from an established aquarium. Sometimes a few small bits of clam are introduced into the aquarium to help speed up the bacterial growth. Unfortunately, although the process is speeded up, the tank gives off a rather bad smell for several days, but with a little patience the tank can be ready for occupation by the fishes in a relatively short time. A tank will have "cured" when the ammonia and nitrite levels have risen to high levels and then have dropped to near zero. A few inexpensive, hardy fishes can be used as starters to see if everything has gone as planned. Damselfishes are a good choice. If they survive, act normally, and eat well, the more delicate and more expensive fishes can be added. It is also best for the beginner to maintain the marine tank with only the inexpensive fishes until he is satisfied that he has the ability to go on to the more challenging fishes.

The biological filtration system is a sort of compromise between two other basic methods of keeping marine fishes, the natural system and the sterile system. The sterile system is not really sterile, but an attempt is made to come as close to sterile as possible. Filtration is of utmost importance, and both box-type and diatom filters are used to keep all impurities out of the tank. Undergravel filters are usually avoided since they promote a bacterial growth leading to biological filtration. All filter media are cleaned often. The result is a crystal-clear aquarium hopefully free from any dirt or disease-causing organisms. Algae, of course, are not encouraged to grow and are removed as soon as they appear. Decorations are kept scrupulously clean. This was the most popular system in the early days of the marine hobby and, in many cases, it worked. The fishes do tend to become pale in such "sterile" conditions, and if anything goes wrong they will die off rather quickly. But there is an

1. *Chaetodon melapterus*.
2. *Chaetodon larvatus*. 3.
Arothron hispidus. 4. *Canthigaster valentini*. 5.
Diodon hystrix, inflated
and deflated. (Photos. 1.
Dr. Warren E. burgess. 2.
CLI. 3. Alan Power. 4. Dr.
G. R. Allen. 5. CLI.

3

4

5

1

2

3

advantage: in the sterile system the tank can be set up and the fishes added almost immediately without aging.

The sterile system is somewhat limiting as to the type of fishes that can be kept. Since the bottom layer of gravel must be very shallow (deeper sand or gravel tends to harbor unwanted organisms), burrowing fishes such as wrasses must be passed by. But on the other hand, if the fishes get sick and must be treated, the medication does not destroy the system (in the biological filtration system it would kill off the bacteria).

Quite opposite to the sterile system is the "natural" system. In this system, developed by Mr. Lee Chin Eng, the tank supports a variety of organisms from fan worms, bivalves, starfishes, coral, and sponges to algae and fishes only by the use of airstones. The filtration is accomplished by natural means, that is by the filter-feeders. There is still controversy over whether the system works or not. Those who have tried it and claim success say it is not difficult; those who have tried it and failed say it cannot be done. Regardless of who is correct, once a system such as that described is set-up and fails, the result is catastrophic and the whole tank must be torn down—a difficult and smelly proposition. In any event, unless an aquarist lives close enough to the water to be able to collect the organisms and the water itself, it should not even be tried.

1. *Pterois volitans*, usually the center of attraction of any marine aquarium. 2. Juvenile angelfishes, like this *Pomacanthus arcuatus*, will pick at living gorgonians for food. 3. Two popular butterflyfishes for the marine aquarium, *Chaetodon meyeri* (above) and *Heniochus acuminatus*. (Photos 1. & 2. R. P. L. Straughan. 3. Wilhelm Hoppe.)

Paracanthurus hepatus, one of the surgeonfishes commonly kept in marine aquaria. Photo by G. Marcuse. Below: The blue-faced angelfish, *Euxiphipops xanthometapon,* is conspicuously patterned in bright colors.

Selecting the Fishes

When choosing fishes it must be remembered that, in general, fewer marine fishes can be kept in a particular sized tank than freshwater fishes in a similar sized tank. This is one of the most important rules of marine fish keeping, and one that is broken most often by both a beginner and a transferee from the freshwater hobby. The beginner wants to start out by keeping every fish he always admired in the store, and the freshwater hobbyist tries to apply the inch-per-gallon method he used successfully with his freshwater tanks to the marine aquaria. It doesn't work. Crowding marine fishes invites disaster. It is probably the single most important cause of problems in a marine tank.

Once the tank has been set up with the water, coral decorations, etc., and the nitrite and ammonia levels are near zero, the tank is said to be aged and is ready to accommodate fishes. It is best to start slowly. A few damselfishes can be used as guinea pigs to test the system to see if it really works. If, after they are added, they remain healthy and active and the chemical composition is not drastically altered, additional species can join them. Always keep one eye on the fishes and the other eye on the chemical conditions. If the pH drops and/or the nitrites or ammonia rises, action must be taken. Increased aeration, water changes, and thorough cleaning are some steps to reverse such a lowering of the pH. It is important to take inventory of the fishes quite often to make sure that if one dies for any reason it is discovered and removed as quickly as possible to prevent pollution.

There are no strict rules to follow when judging how many fishes an aquarium can hold. This depends to a great deal on the species of fishes kept, their rate of growth, the conditions in the tank, how many and what type of fishes are to be added, and how experienced the aquarist is. A very rough estimate to start with is about one 1″-2″ fish per five gallons. This takes into account that the fishes are bound to grow larger with proper care. Thus, when the fishes double their size to 2″-4″, the five gallons will still be sufficient. In a 50-gallon tank, then, ten fishes of 1″-2″ length will do very well, with allowance for growth already taken into account. Although the figures may be juggled to some extent, for instance adding a couple of larger fishes but subtracting some of the smaller ones to compensate, they should not be abused. A more advanced marine aquarist might be able to squeeze about fifteen 1″-2″ fishes into the same 50-gallon tank, or maybe ten 4″ fishes, five 6″ fishes, or one or two fishes larger than 7″.

The amount of crowding depends a lot upon the type of

THE WORLD'S LARGEST SELECTION OF PET, ANIMAL, AND MUSIC BOOKS.

T.F.H. Publications publishes more than 900 books covering many hobby aspects (dogs, cats, birds, fish, small animals, music, etc.). Whether you are a beginner or an advanced hobbyist you will find exactly what you're looking for among our complete listing of books. For a free catalog fill out the form on the other side of this page and mail it today.

. . . CATS . . .

. . . BIRDS . .

. . . ANIMALS . . .

. . . DOGS . . .

. . FISH . . .

. . . MUSIC . . .

For more than 30 years, *Tropical Fish Hobbyist* has been the source of accurate, up-to-the-minute, and fascinating information on every facet of the aquarium hobby.

Join the more than 50,000 devoted readers worldwide who wouldn't miss a single issue.

species kept. For instance, the hardier damselfishes can be crowded more safely than, say, butterflyfishes. The various types of fishes will be covered in more detail in later chapters.

Only young, healthy fishes should be chosen. Most dealers will gladly help in the selection of fishes, giving advice about which ones are compatible, which ones are acting normally, and which ones are feeding properly. If the aquarist must rely on his own judgment, however, there are certain things to look for. The fish must be alert and active (if that is its nature). If there are several fish in a tank and all appear healthy except one or two that may be off-color and lethargic or even hiding in a corner, those two must in all events be avoided and the others held in suspicion until it is ascertained whether or not what is affecting the two abnormal ones can be or has been transferred to the apparently healthy ones. The gill movements can be checked to see if they are overly rapid, an indication of some form of trouble (including parasitic infestation of the gills). They should be regular and relatively slow unless the fish has been frightened by your presence or other reasons, in which case the rapid gill movements (breathing) can be attributed to fright.

The color of the fish should be good, not faded out or darkened and blotchy (sometimes fright characteristics). It should not be too intense, as many times the color of a fish will shine most brilliantly just before death. The fins should be moving normally, not clamped to the side. A knowledge of the species is necessary here because it is important to know which fishes normally carry their fins erect and which normally carry them folded. Some wrasses, for example, swim with their pectoral fins while holding the dorsal and anal fins closed until they are needed for maneuvering.

There should be no signs of disease on the fish. Each individual should be closely inspected for spots, sores, hemorrhaging, and watched for unusual behavior such as scratching or disorientation.

The fishes should be eating well and neither bloated nor thin and hollow-bellied. A dealer will often gladly place some food in the tank to prove that his fishes are healthy and eating well. If the fishes were just fed and show no further interest in food, perhaps a demonstration can be arranged for the next day. Sometimes new arrivals are shy about feeding at first, but with a little bit of coaxing they will eventually come out at feeding time for their share. If the aquarist himself is inexperienced in coaxing new fishes to start eating, it may be best to wait until the dealer has them "started" before purchasing them.

If there is any doubt about the condition of the fishes, it might be preferable to wait and watch them over a period of time in the dealer's tanks. Once satisfied with their condition, the aquarist can then safely take them home. If there is a possibility that the fishes might be sold, perhaps a deposit might persuade the dealer to hold them for a week or so.

Aside from the general health of the fishes, the aquarist must be concerned about their compatibility. It certainly is not very intelligent to place several small fishes in the tank with a large predatory species. It would not be very long (sometimes only seconds) before the smaller individuals start disappearing down the gullet of the larger fish. Neither is it recommended to place members of the same species together when they are the type that will constantly fight each other, such as small French or gray angelfishes. If death does not result from the constant scrimmaging, torn or tattered fins probably will. The dealer again is one source of information as to which fishes are truly compatible with one another. It can surely be noticed that some species in a dealer's tanks are placed together with no problems whereas other species are placed one to a tank. If the dealer won't place them together, the aquarist should be warned that he, too, should not.

Fishes that are collected by the aquarist in the wild for his newly set-up tank should also be carefully selected. It is often too tempting to collect everything in sight and bring it all home only to discover that there are too many fishes for the size tank or that the fishes are not compatible. Either all the fishes are dumped in the tank anyway, leading to all sorts of problems and eventual death of many if not all of the fishes, or they must be culled, either by giving away the extras (if possible) or destroying them. The best method would be to collect only those fishes which will safely be housed in the set-up tank or, if the thrill of the hunt has caused an excess of fishes to be collected, the extras should be released where they were caught.

Some fishes, such as these young *Pomacanthus arcuatus,* are scrappy. Here a small one is being chased by a larger individual. Photo by Marine Aquarium Products.

Chaetodon ephippium juvenile. Butterflyfishes are rather delicate and care must be taken when introducing them to the home aquarium. Photo by G. Marcuse. Large groupers, like the *Cephalopholis miniatus* shown below, adapt well and soon will be looking for small fishes to devour. Photo by G. Marcuse.

Introducing The New Fishes

If care is taken when setting up the tank to match the water chemistry with that of the dealer's tanks, few problems will be encountered when bringing newly purchased fishes home. All that has to be done is to take a quick check of the temperature to make sure that there is no great difference between the bag water and the tank water. It is also advisable to test the two water chemistries once more just to make sure nothing has gone awry since the last tests. It is to be expected that the pH level will drop a bit in the transportation bag, especially if the fishes are carried over a relatively long distance, due to the accumulation of feces from the frightened fishes and their respiration (utilization of oxygen and giving off CO_2).

For naturally collected fishes or fishes from water in a dealer's tanks in which the chemistry is not known, it is best to run the full series of tests on the water to see how different the source is from the new tank. If the differences are great a period of acclimation must take place before the fishes can be placed in their new home. Too many times new fishes are unceremoniously dumped into the tank because of time problems or just plain ignorance, only to see them immediately go into shock. Although some fishes eventually recover from shock, others never do. Those that do not go into shock may have their resistance lowered to such an extent that they are easy victims of any disease organisms present.

If the temperature and/or chemistry of the bag water and tank water differ greatly, adjustments must be made to decrease the possibility of shock due to the change. Upward changes (raising the temperature, increasing the density, etc.) can be made faster than downward changes. Naturally, due to the comparative volumes of water, changes in the bag water are more easily effected than those in the tank water.

Floating the bag in the tank, such as done with freshwater fishes, works well for small temperature changes. If the bag temperature is cool but within the normal temperature range, warming it at the rate of 2°F/day is recommended. Sudden upward changes should never exceed 5°F, nor should downward changes exceed 3°F. If the bag has been chilled and the temperature is below the normal limits, more rapid warming can not only take place but is recommended, the chilly water causing more damage than the sudden rise in temperature.

Changes in pH can best be achieved by adding some tank water to the bag at intervals while removing a similar amount of bag water to keep the level even. The rate of change should not exceed 0.2/day.

Changes in the specific gravity can be accomplished in the same way at the same time. Replacing a little bit of bag water with tank water will effect the changes without undo strain on the fishes. It is recommended that the change be no more than about 0.0025/day.

Sometimes situations arise in which the recommendations cannot be adhered to. For example, when the fishes have to travel over a long distance or the transportation time is extended because of some unforseen delays, the oxygen may be depleted and the CO_2 built up to such an extent that the fishes are gasping at the surface. The aquarist cannot afford to take the time to adjust the temperature and chemistry of the bag water to the tank water. It comes down to the lesser of several evils—if the fishes will surely die if left in the bag, they must be placed in the tank immediately. Some losses may occur, but at least the fishes have a fighting chance for survival. Sometimes the addition of an airstone to the bag will buy the time needed for a more gradual change, but each situation must be judged individually depending upon the circumstances and handled accordingly.

When exchanging water in the bag for water from the tank, the bag water should be discarded. Eventually the fish should be in almost pure tank water in the bag and can be "floated" out gently without recourse to a net. The less handling of the fishes the better. Picking out a fish by hand is often detrimental to the fish as some of its protective mucous covering will be rubbed off as it often is during contact with a net. Contact with certain fishes can be just as detrimental to the aquarist if the fishes happen to possess sharp spines (sometimes poisonous) or sharp or crushing teeth. If the fish is transferred in a net its spines may sometimes get entangled in its mesh. The fish will often be able to free itself if both fish and net are placed under water, otherwise it must be freed by hand. If damage to the fish is suspected because of this handling, the tank should be dosed with one of the antibiotic and antifungal medicines.

Once placed in the tank, the new fishes must be watched closely for signs of discomfort or for signs of fighting if they have adjusted immediately to their new surroundings.

If the fishes are to be added to an already established tank, additional problems must be taken into consideration. There is always a possibility of their carrying disease organisms or parasites into the tank. For this reason it is best to keep them in a quarantine tank for a period of time in order to keep them under observation. It has been recommended that they be treated with something like copper or potassium permanganate while under quarantine to help eradicate whatever disease organisms or parasites they may have. By the end of a week or two, if no sign of any problem is seen, they can be added to the established tank.

Unfortunately, most people do not have the facilities to set up a quarantine or hospital tank. In that case the fishes must be added directly to the old tank, with all the risks involved. These risks can be reduced considerably if, with every new introduction of fishes, the old tank is dosed with the copper or permanganate solutions.

The fishes to be added to an established aquarium must be chosen with the same care as those that were initially selected for the tank—perhaps even more care, especially if the first residents were territorial. The new additions are bound to be frightened or weakened from their ordeal of being caught in a net, transported in a plastic bag, and placed in entirely new surroundings. They fall easy victim to fishes with established territories who see the new arrivals as intruders and move quickly to attack them. This is compounded by the fact that the new arrivals will make a dash for the nearest cover, which undoubtedly will be part of the territory of one of the old inhabitants. This problem can often be easily solved by shifting the coral decorations around, effectively destroying the territories of the older residents and placing all the fishes, new and old alike, on an equal basis.

It must also be remembered that the new fishes to be added must be compatible both in size and temperament to the older ones. It has happened, though thankfully not often, that new small fishes added to an old tank which housed some larger fishes were treated as if they were feeder guppies and chased down unmercifully until caught and eaten. This is a tremendous shock to the aquarist, especially if the new fishes were of the expensive kind. The reverse could also happen. A new large fish (such as a lionfish) when added to a tank of small fishes might, as soon as the initial shock of introduction wears off, start to deplete the old population just as fast as they could be caught.

The older residents of a tank can be fed before the introduction of new fishes, making them less apt to consider the new additions as supper and allowing time for the new fishes to become a bit acclimated before the next feeding time. In old or new tanks it is not advisable to immediately feed new fishes, but allow them some time to settle down and get over their initial fright or shyness.

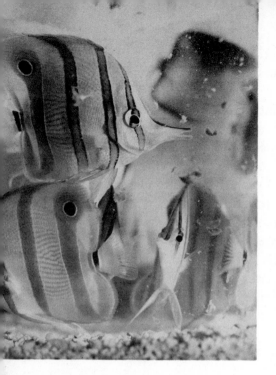

A group of *Chelmon rostratus* avidly snapping up some frozen brine shrimp. Photo by Dr. Anthony Y. F. Teh. Below: *Pterois volitans* will readily consume smaller fishes—whether you want them to or not! Photo by R. P. L. Straughan.

Feeding Marine Fishes

If the beginner has followed the advice in this book and selected only those fishes which he observed feeding in the dealer's tanks, he should have no feeding problems. The dealer will be able to supply him with the same foods that the fishes were eating, and their diet will not change appreciably. The aquarist can try additional, perhaps more nutritious, foods which the dealer, because of time or economy, does not feed his fishes. In case the fishes do not take to the additional foods, the aquarist can still fall back on the items that were being fed beforehand.

With the great expansion of the marine hobby the demand for newer and better foods for marine fishes has resulted in a good variety of frozen, freeze-dried, flake, dried, and live foods being available to the dealer and therefore to the hobbyist. Instead of having to make a selection from the array of foods for freshwater fishes, the marine hobbyist has available to him a similar array of foods designed especially for his marine fishes.

The basic food for use in marine aquaria happens to be, however, one of the staples of the freshwater aquarist: brine shrimp. Because these little creatures are more adapted to salt water than to fresh water, the marine hobbyist has a distinct advantage. The brine shrimp, when fed alive, will not die as quickly in marine water as in fresh water and any overfeeding will be minimized. In fact, a few extra brine shrimp in the water will often ensure that all fishes will get something to eat since some of the more timid individuals may hide when the aquarist is standing at the tank putting the food in.

Brine shrimp also comes frozen and freeze-dried, both forms being readily accepted by the majority of marine fishes. In addition, frozen clams, shrimps, squid, etc. are packaged for the use of marine aquarists who wish to vary their charges' diet as much as possible. These foods can be fed in bite-sized portions depending upon the size of the fishes being fed. In some packages vegetable matter in the form of algae or kelp is added to help provide a more balanced diet for some omnivorous or herbivorous fishes. For larger individuals whole shrimp or prawn, as well as pieces of fish and squid, are usually available.

Marine flake food, which is guaranteed not to pollute the water, is available and has become one of the staples for marine fishes. It has the advantage of being a better balanced food than most others. Thus, even if live foods are not available there are enough prepared foods to provide most marine fishes with an adequate diet. In a pinch the marine aquarist can always fall back on some freshwater foods such as *Daphnia*, *Tubifex* worms, white worms, etc.

Many fishes have very interesting or peculiar feeding habits and, although they will eat what is offered, they will often put on a great show if fed natural live foods. The frogfishes, for instance, will eat pieces of fish or shrimp that fall or are placed near them, but if live minnows or other similar small fishes are placed in their tank they will "angle" for them. They have the first dorsal spine modified into a sort of fishing pole, complete with worm-like lure. This lure or bait is waved about in the water to attract one of the small fishes into the vicinity, thinking it will be getting something to eat. When the small fish comes close enough to the frogfish it is quickly snapped up. Lionfishes (*Pterois* spp.), when fed with live foods such as small fishes, will use their large pectoral fins to corral their prey. It is a truly fascinating sight to see them stalking their intended victims. On the other hand, moray eels will take a small squid (usually dangled in front of their noses) into their mouth and then literally tie themselves into knots as they proceed to swallow it. Parrotfishes and many surgeonfishes are algae-scrapers and usually clean off the aquarium walls just as fast as they become covered with a growth of algae.

Among the more difficult fishes to feed are the butterflyfishes. These delicate fishes have small mouths with rows of slender teeth like a brush which are used to feed on corals or to scrape up some of the benthic invertebrates that live on the corals and rocks of their environment. Although some individuals learn to accept brine shrimp and other such morsels, many will shun all types of foods until they eventually die from starvation. One trick used to try and start them feeding is to smear some brine shrimp or other frozen food on a piece of coral. The butterflyfish can pick at the coral (which is its natural method of feeding) and get some nourishment in return. Once it is accepting this type of food from the coral, it is often a short step to accepting it directly.

Natural foods collected from the nearby ocean should usually be avoided. There is no way of telling what parasites or diseases they will be carrying into the marine tank. If the aquarist is willing to take the risk, however, he should select small rocks covered with a good growth of organisms but free from bottom sediment, dying organisms, etc. These can be placed in the tank for short periods of time and the inhabitants of the tank allowed to pick them over. After a short period of time, or when the rock is picked clean, it can be removed. Never leave it in for any length of time. Small seines or hand nets will often turn up shrimps, crabs, fishes, etc. that may be suitable for feeding. It might be advisable to dose them with copper or permanganate solution before using them for food.

The fishes in a marine aquarium should be fed sparingly but often. Several feedings a day of mixed fare is excellent. Brine shrimp, live if possible, and marine flake foods can be the basic foods for every feeding, with additions of other items such as clams, shrimp, fish, etc. on a rotating basis. Care should be taken not to overfeed or underfeed. Overfeeding usually means scraps of uneaten food getting hidden in small niches about the coral, eventually decaying and possibly causing problems. After feeding, siphon out most of the untouched food—the little that is left will usually be finished off in a few minutes as some fishes get their "second wind." Underfeeding causes the fishes to become thin and weakened and prone to all sorts of infestations by parasites and diseases. With time the aquarist will be able to judge how much food should be fed and which fishes need individual attention (in case some of the larger or swifter fishes are hogging all the food). Generally, each feeding should last 5-10 minutes, depending of course upon how many fishes are in the tank, how fast they can capture and devour the food, and what type food is being fed.

The timing of the feedings is also important, depending upon the species of fishes kept. Some species feed only in the daytime, others only at night. It is important to know which type fishes are in the aquarium and to time the feedings accordingly.

Movement of the food is often important to some of the more reluctant feeders. They normally take only live food (which is moving) but sometimes can be coaxed into accepting some of the frozen food if it is placed in the current from a filter or airstone. This artificial motion is often enough to entice the hungry fish to snap it up. Food that is ignored once it settles on the bottom can be siphoned up and replaced in the currents for another try. Some foods can even be placed on the end of a stick and wiggled in front of the nose of reluctant fishes. The artificial movement is often enough to precipitate a strike at the object by the fish. Once the fish becomes acclimated to the taste and smell, the stick can be dispensed with and the food even delivered by hand. This is often the case with lionfishes.

Moray eels can be started with food placed on the end of a stick. Photo by Tierney & Killingsworth.

A *Dascyllus trimaculatus* with its fins damaged, leaving the door open for fungus or other infections. Photo by Laurence E. Perkins. The *Calloplesiops altivelis* individual shown below has an infected area around its eyes. If the infection spreads the fish could go blind. Photo by G. Marcuse.

Diseases and Parasites

Although our knowledge of marine aquarium fish diseases and parasites has increased tremendously in recent years, it still is hopelessly inadequate when trying to diagnose and cure the ailments that strike a marine hobbyist's tanks. There is still much more guesswork and luck in treating the various problems than actual premeditated cures. With the new techniques and equipment the incidence of disease in marine tanks has dropped significantly but unmanageable problems still arise too often. Even the experienced marine aquarist is not immune to the ravages of disease no matter how fastidiously he cares for his fishes. This may be partly due to the fact that a fish may not show any symptoms of a disease yet be a "carrier." This fish can unsuspectingly be placed in an aquarium where it transmits the disease to the other fishes without being affected itself.

The marine tank is an unnatural environment for captive fishes and as such places them in a stressful situation. This stress helps prevent the fishes from successfully fighting off many of the organisms that are ever-present in the tank. These stresses on a fish are basically due to the chemical and physical fluctuations that they do not normally encounter in their natural habitat and the unnatural diets they are forced to rely upon, in many cases inadequate as far as proper nutrition is concerned. In addition, in a marine tank the fishes are kept in close contact continuously so that if one succumbs to a disease the others most likely will follow suit.

Another situation that arises in the marine aquarium is placing together in one enclosed space fishes with entirely different spectrums as far as disease susceptibility and resistance are concerned. The "carrier" mentioned above might be a carrier because it has developed a certain amount of immunity to that disease in the area from which it comes. Its tankmates, however, coming from different areas, may not have been exposed to the same disease and have no resistance to it whatsoever, so they contract it.

The best defenses an aquarist has against the array of diseases and parasites which can attack his fishes are a well-kept aquarium, a nutritious balanced diet, and unrelenting attention to the behavior and appearance of his fishes and the chemical and physical properties of his aquarium water. A properly kept tank with strong, healthy fishes does not guarantee that there will never be troubles, but it does greatly reduce the chances that something will happen.

Unfortunately, it is a rare aquarist who has been able to keep fishes (and this can probably be said for many freshwater aquarists as well) for some length of time without running into some difficulties with parasites and diseases. It is the well-informed aquarist, able to recognize trouble early, who stands the best chance of combating it and saving his fishes. An aquarist should not be discouraged by the long and complicated scientific names of disease organisms floating around. As long as he is able to judge whether the infection in his fishes happens to be of bacterial, viral, protozoan, etc. origin and can therefore choose the proper type of treatment, the situation can usually be brought under control. In other words, it is quite useless to dose the tank with medication for a bacterial infection when the fishes happen to be suffering from a protozoan disease.

Among the most common of the marine fish diseases are the white spot diseases. They are basically of two types, one with very tiny white spots that are almost velvety in appearance (this disease is often distinguished from the other white spot disease and called velvet disease) and another in which the white spots are somewhat larger. Velvet disease is caused by a ciliated protozoan called *Oodinium ocellatum* (sometimes referred to as *Amblyoodinium ocellatum*), whereas the white spot disease is caused by another protozoan called *Cryptocaryon irritans*. In both instances the small white spots are difficult to see and must be viewed under the correct lighting. The two diseases are difficult to distinguish although the white spots in the white spot disease are a bit larger than those in velvet. The treatment is generally the same, so distinction between the two is not absolutely necessary.

In both cases the symptoms are the same: increased respiration (as evidenced by the gill movements); hovering near the surface of the tank while breathing rapidly; scratching or scraping movements (flashing) against objects in the tank; clamped fins; and shimmying. The gills are almost always attacked first, so the diseases may not be evident until they have gained a considerable foothold on the fish. Each tiny white spot is a potential source for hundreds of new organisms, each with the capability of infecting the fish and in turn producing hundreds more. It is not definitely known whether the multiplication occurs while

51

the cyst is on the fish or after it drops off and falls to the bottom of the tank, but this really doesn't matter to the aquarist, who treats the infection the same way regardless.

For velvet or white spot disease the basic treatment is copper. This must be administered over a period of about two weeks so that the protozoan, which matures on the fish (in this encysted stage the copper cannot directly affect it), can be killed off in its free-swimming infective stage. The protozoan matures in about ten days, but this period can be shortened by raising the temperature a bit. Copper sulphate should be added to the tank until the concentration reaches a level between 0.15-0.4ppm after the activated charcoal from the filter, coral, shells, and other decorations are removed. There is a controversy as to whether or not the biological filter should or should not be discontinued for the treatment. It may be best to keep it running to try and maintain the tank at previous chemical levels since a buildup of toxic wastes might harm the fishes in their weakened condition. Constantly monitor the copper level in the tank and add more when it is needed. Copper treatment kits are now available that will not only provide the aquarist with the necessary directions of application but also provide means by which the concentrations can be tested. In general, a 1% copper sulphate solution administered in a dosage of 1 ml for each four gallons is recommended for the sterile system (more for the biological filtration system). Invertebrates and algae should be removed from the tank prior to the administration of the copper as it is very toxic to these organisms. After the two weeks of treatment the corals, other invertebrates, etc. can be replaced *providing* (1) all spots have disappeared along with all the other symptoms, and (2) all traces of the copper are gone from the tank.

Both overdosing and underdosing a tank can be dangerous. Underdosing (possibly caused by absorption of the copper by various items in the tank) naturally will allow the disease to continue in the tank, eventually killing the fishes; overdosing will harm the fishes. The fishes affected by too much copper become disoriented (falling on their sides) and gasp excessively. Feed the fishes sparingly during the treatment.

Both white spot diseases are very contagious. If a new fish that is infected or is a carrier is added to the tank, chances are the disease will spread very rapidly, infecting most or all of the other fishes. Once the disease is detected, be careful with aquarium equipment such as nets that might transfer some of the disease organisms to another tank and start another epidemic.

Sodium sulphathiazole has been found to be effective against white spot (not velvet) and is considerably safer where invertebrates are concerned.

Bacterial infections should be suspected in fishes with frayed or eroded fins (so-called fin-rot and tail-rot), reddened areas at the base of the fins, around the mouth (sometimes called mouth fungus but really not a fungus), and along the lateral line, and exophthalmus (pop-eye) in the later stages. Most bacterial infections can be treated with a broad-spectrum antibiotic such as Oxytetracycline (Terramycin), chloromycetin, one of the sulfa drugs, or one of the penicillin group. These drugs are best administered internally, which entails getting the fishes to eat food which has some of the bacteriacides mixed in with it. If this fails the whole tank must be treated and the dosages correspondingly increased (about 50mg/gallon compared to about 0.1-1.0% when given in the diet).

The wasting disease (tuberculosis) may be suspected when the fishes become listless and stop eating (usually resulting in an emaciated or hollow-bellied appearance). The fins become frayed, lesions appear on the skin as well as the fins, exophthalmus may occur, and the general color becomes poor or blotchy. Although tuberculosis is a bacterial infection, the broad spectrum antibiotics listed above do not seem to be as effective in this disease. Isoniazid is recommended in a dosage of 250mg/5 gallons of water. After every three days 25% of the water should be replaced with new water while adding an additional 200mg of isoniazid/5 gallons. Continue the treatment for up to 60 days.

Fungal infections *(Saprolegnia)* may readily be recognized as white cotton-like lesions on the fins or body. It does not attack healthy tissue but finds a foothold on dead or dying tissues such as damaged fins or spots where the mucus of the body has been rubbed off by rough handling with a net or the aquarist's hands. Fungus can easily be treated by direct application to the infected area of substances such as hydrogen peroxide, 2% Mercurochrome, iodine (a 10% solution of the commercial variety), malachite green, etc. In addition to the swabbing of the infected area, a general treatment of Furanace (1 capsule/10 gallons) is recommended to combat any internal infection.

Lymphocystis is a viral disease evidenced by wart-like lesions occurring on the fish's body in the form of pimples or nodules or even larger cauliflower-like growths. These growths are composed of swollen connective tissue and usually affect individual fishes rather than spread throughout the tank in epidemic form, at least at first. The virus is contagious and is usually passed to other fishes that ingest pieces of the nodules that flake off or, if the infected fish dies, by nibbling at the infected parts. The infected fish must be removed before the disease spreads and kept in quarantine for a period of about two months. There is no known remedy, but the natural resistance of the fish will often overcome the disease and the fish will recover spontaneously.

The gasping syndrome (fishes in the tank start to breathe rapidly, gasp for air with opercles flared wide, swim irregularly, etc.) and anoxia (fishes die with mouth wide open, opercles flared causing the pale gills to be visible) have in common the lack of adequate oxygen supplies. The gasping syndrome can be caused by overcrowding, inadequate aeration, some poisonous substance in the water, or overly high temperatures (possibly caused by a defective thermostat). Aeration must be increased immediately and as much as of the water changed as feasible; the nitrites should be tested and the temperature checked. A thorough cleaning of the tank is in order, and the population should be thinned out if it has grown too large.

For anoxia, much the same "treatment" can be applied: increase the oxygen supply, thin out the tank if it is overcrowded, check for dead fishes or rotting uneaten food, and change as much of the water as possible.

Exophthalmus is more of a symptom than a disease itself and may appear in conjunction with several bacterial, fungal, or viral diseases as well as being caused by an overdose of copper. Treatment of the accompanying disease will usually alleviate the exophthalmus as well except in cases where copper was the villain. In this last situation reduction of the amount of copper in the water usually has a beneficial effect.

Parasites can often be seen on the fishes as they are inspected closely before purchase. However, some parasites may remain undetected (especially those in hidden places such as the gills) and eventually cause problems in the aquarium. It would be nice to be able to keep some cleaner wrasses in the aquarium to pick off these unwanted pests (as well as diseased tissues which might otherwise be subject to fungus infection), but this is not practical as once the aquarium residents are cleaned of all their parasites the wrasses would die of starvation. The parasitized fishes can be bathed in fresh water of the same temperature and pH for a period not exceeding three minutes in an attempt to remove the parasites. If this fails a bath in a formaldehyde

1. *Acanthurus olivaceus* with a bad infection. 2. *Pomacanthus semicirculatus* with a white spot disease. 3. *Labroides dimidiatus* removing parasites from *Chaetodon collare*. (Photos. 1. G. Marcuse. 2. W. Hoppe. 3. H. Hansen.)

2

solution (1 ml of concentrated formalin per gallon of salt) can be tried. The fishes can be placed in this bath for up to 30 minutes.

Unusual behavior of the fishes in a marine tank, such as gasping or disorientation, might be attributable to toxic conditions caused by foreign substances being dropped into the tank (during house cleaning, spraying, painting, etc.) or entering the tank via the aeration system. Pump intakes may be sucking in fumes from paint, insecticides, tobacco, etc., causing it to be forced into the tank through the airstones. And of course an aquarist placing his hands in the tank might be introducing toxic substances (caught under the fingernails for instance) to it.

3

The jewelfish, *Microspathodon chrysurus,* is very aggressive and does very well in home aquaria. Photo by N.Y. Zoological Society. Below: *Balistoides conspicillum* is relatively hardy but has a high initial cost. Photo by Klaus Paysan.

Fishes Suitable For The Marine Aquarium

Undoubtedly there are thousands of marine fishes which would be suitable for the home aquarium. Obviously not all of them can be contained in a limited sized book such as this one. The fishes to be treated in the following pages are those, then, that are most available to the marine aquarist. They range from the rather bizarre seahorses to the elegant Moorish idol, from the delicate beauty of the butterflyfishes to the large and powerful groupers, and from the beautiful but dangerous lionfishes to the anemone-inhabiting clownfishes.

SEAHORSES

One of the most unusual creatures kept in home marine aquaria is the seahorse. It is almost hard to believe that it is truly a fish. It has its head at right angles to the body, a long prehensile tail, and everything encased in a bony armor. Most of its time is spent with the tail wrapped around some holdfast such as a piece of branching coral or blade of grass (in nature) waiting for a tidbit of food to go drifting by. If by any chance they leave their perch, they move slowly about the tank propelled by the small dorsal fin in the middle of their back. This locomotion is by no means fast enough to capture live food that is able to dodge its advances, but adequate enough to get it from one position to perhaps a better one where food is more apt to pass by. In an aquarium live brine shrimp are an excellent food, and many an aquarist has been able to maintain seahorses on this diet alone. Larger seahorses have been tempted with live baby guppies (if they could catch them) and were even trained to accept them by hand.

Because of the slowness of their locomotion, seahorses should not be kept with other fishes. There is no way, unless they are hand-fed, that seahorses can compete for food with any of the faster swimming fishes.

One very unusual characteristic of seahorses is that it is the male which gives birth to the living young. Actually the female deposits her eggs in a specially constructed brood pouch in the male where they are fertilized and undergo development. This brood pouch is also an excellent way in which to recognize the sexes, the male having it, the female without it. Mating and delivery of the baby seahorses has occurred commonly in aquaria, making the keeping of these fishes so much more desirable. The male brood pouch swells as the babies develop until it seems it will burst. . .and it almost appears to burst as he goes through the "agonies" of delivery. The babies, tiny replicas of the parents, are popped out one or several at a time into the surrounding water. They swim off in their feeble way until they encounter a slender holdfast around which they can wrap their already prehensile tail. There they hang on and wait for food (in the aquarium in the form of newly hatched brine shrimp) to come within reach. They then snap up each morsel in a lightning-fast strike coupled with a sudden suction caused by the expansion of the gill covers.

Seahorses mostly belong to the genus *Hippocampus* and range in size from the 1″ dwarf seahorse to the larger 7″-8″ species. Although most of the species of seahorses look similar, some, especially those from Australia and their close relatives the sea dragons *(Phallopteryx, Phycoduras,* etc.), may sport leafy appendages and bright colors.

The related pipefishes *(Syngnathus* spp., etc.) lack the angled head and prehensile tail and, although they have been kept in marine aquaria, do not have the tremendous popularity of the seahorses.

LIONFISHES

Most of the members of the family Scorpaenidae are not kept in marine aquaria. They are often quite sedentary, not very beautiful, and have large mouths which are used for engulfing small unsuspecting fishes. Most are provided with poisonous spines in the dorsal fin and around the head, and a few species, collectively called stonefishes, have a venom which is very potent and in some cases has been reported to cause human deaths.

There are a few genera, the most popular of which is *Pterois,* that are not only kept by marine aquarists but are favorites among them. These lionfishes are generally brightly colored in shades of brown, red, tan, and white, with very large, feathery pectoral fins. They glide around the tank in a sedate manner, appearing confident that they are the rulers of the tank, no fish daring to defy them. They are also predatory, and any fishes small enough to fit into the large mouth will be hunted down and eaten. This hunting process involves the large pectoral fins, which are said to be used to herd the prey into a corner where it is trapped.

Lionfishes have the same poisonous dorsal spines as their relatives and should be handled with care. They can be fed with small live fishes (guppies are a favorite) to start and eventually with small bits of frozen fish, squid, or other chunk-style foods. Lionfishes are hardy and do not easily fall victim to common aquarium diseases.

DAMSELFISHES AND ANEMONEFISHES

If any marine fishes can be said to be the "basic" or "standard" fishes for the marine aquarium, it would be the members of the family Pomacentridae, known to aquarists as the damselfishes and anemonefishes. Almost as a group they are hardy, small, adapt well to aquarium life, and are inexpensive as marines go. These are generally the first fishes placed in a new tank to test the conditions for suitability for the more delicate fishes. The family is normally divided into the damselfishes proper (*Pomacentrus, Abudefduf, Chromis,* etc.) and the anemonefishes (*Amphiprion* and *Premnas*). Somewhere in between are the popular humbugs of the genus *Dascyllus.*

Damselfishes comprise by far the greatest number of species in the family. They come in a vast array of colors, some a bit somber but others brilliant in glowing neon hues. All seem to be highly adaptable to life in an aquarium, where they stake out a corner or particular stand of coral as their own. This territory is jealously guarded from all intruders, especially those of their own species. They are very "busy" in the tank, darting about here and there inspecting, picking fights, or fleeing from aggressors (but only temporarily). They are easily cared for and will withstand more fluctuations in chemical and physical conditions than most other fishes that are commonly kept in marine aquaria. Food is no problem, as they will accept almost any type of prepared aquarium foods. Brine shrimp (live, frozen, freeze-dried, etc.), flake foods, bloodworms, mosquito larvae, chopped clams, shrimp, and beef-heart or other lean meat are all taken by damselfishes without much hesitation.

Anemonefishes are a special group of pomacentrids that have become adapted to life among the stinging tentacles of sea anemones (hence their name). There are only about 26 species, all colored in oranges, reds, tans, pinks, brown, black, and white, and many with trimmings and reflections of blue. The patterns of stripes are usually enough to distinguish the different species.

These anemonefishes at an early stage in their life become adapted to living among the tentacles of sea anemones. They develop an immunity to the stings through controlled contact with the tentacles but may lose it if their body slime is removed (as through rough handling). Observations on some young anemonefishes, as well as older fish not adapted to a particular anemone in a tank, indicate that the anemonefish will approach the anemone *tail first*. As they back into the anemone and the first contact with the tentacles is made, they quickly dart away, apparently stung. Since the sting is on a less delicate part of the body, the tail, there is no damage done. The fish will then repeat the process, jumping away as contact is made again. The process is repeated several times until there is no more violent reaction by the fish. At this point the immunity has been built up to such a level that the fish can enter the anemone without being stung. They can then swim about among the tentacles without causing the stinging nematocysts to discharge, although another fish coming in contact with these same tentacles will immediately be stung. This effectively provides some protection for the anemonefishes, which will remain safely among the tentacles when danger threatens.

The humbugs, or members of the damselfish genus, *Dascyllus,* are favorites with marine aquarists. Most sport patterns of black and white—some with spots, some with bars, many with a touch of yellow or blue. These fishes are found more often around stands of coral rather than anemones, but they have been known to become acclimated to existence in an anemone like the anemonefishes. In nature a small school will often be seen hovering above a stand of coral picking at passing plankton. At the approach of danger they will settle among the coral branches, using the sharp coral as a deterrent to an attack. As the danger passes the fishes again can be seen above the coral. Similar behavior can be seen in the home aquarium. They will be out and about the tank if not bothered but will hide among the branches of the coral decorations if disturbed or frightened in any way.

Anemonefishes and humbugs will accept the same foods eaten by the damselfishes.

Pomacentrids tend to be aggressive, and tankmates should be chosen with this in mind. Their small size usually prevents them from doing much damage, except perhaps toward members of their own kind. They make good community fishes if kept with species somewhat larger than themselves.

TRIGGERFISHES, TRUNKFISHES, PUFFERS and PORCUPINEFISHES

These families (along with a few others not normally kept in home aquaria) are collectively called plectognaths. Each family is unusual in its own way, but they have enough characters in common to cause scientists to group them together in their own order.

Triggerfishes are unique in having the dorsal fin spines modified to form a locking device. When the spines are erect they cannot be folded back down again by the aquarist without breaking them, unless he knows their secret. The unlocking mechanism concerns the small third spine which, when depressed, releases the second and first spines so they can easily be folded back. This is a protective device. When triggerfishes hide in a coral hole and lock their spines erect they cannot be budged. To remove a holed-up triggerfish from his tank the aquarist must first unlock the trigger, fold it down, and then pull the fish out from its hiding place.

Triggerfishes are very hardy but usually unsociable. They have sharp crunching teeth which are used, in some species, to crack open the solid tests of sea urchins. These teeth can also inflict serious damage to tankmates that cannot find a suitable hiding place or flee fast enough from the triggers. They especially like to battle each other, so it is recommended that two triggerfishes, at least of the same species, should not be kept together. Those that are kept should be small (1"-2") unless the tank is very large and the fishes contained in it are fast enough or tough enough to hold their own with the triggers.

One of the most sought-after triggerfishes, a favorite of almost every marine aquarist, is the clown trigger, *Balistoides conspicillum*. Recently small specimens have been appearing for sale, much to the delight of everyone. They are hardy and grow quickly, making it imperative that enough tank space is devoted to them.

Trunkfishes are unique in having the body encased in an armor of modified scales. For this protection the fishes must give up speed. Some species are so slow-swimming that they can even be caught by hand. Their main propulsion is derived from the tail fin and small dorsal, anal, and pectoral fins which more or less stick out from this hard box-like encasement.

Trunkfishes are not difficult to care for, and small individuals make a very interesting addition to a marine tank. They pick at their food with their small mouths and will readily accept such large items as chopped fish, clam, shrimp, etc. along with the smaller brine shrimp which can be swallowed whole. As long as they are "happy" there is

1

2

3

4

1. *Holacanthus ciliaris* juvenile from Florida and the Caribbean. 2. *Holacanthus passer* juvenile from the western coast of Mexico. 3. *Pomacanthus paru* attacking its image while two damsels, *Eupomacentrus dorsopunicans* (flame-back damsel) and *E. leucostictus* (beau gregory) stand by. 4. A young *Euxiphipops navarchus*. (Photos. 1. Dr. Gerald R. Allen. 2. A. Kerstitch. 3. CLI. 4. Aaron Norman.

no problem. Some species, however, when placed in a stressful situation will exude a toxic substance. This has caused many losses in bags used to transport them along with other fishes and in tanks in which something has gone wrong.

Puffers and porcupinefishes are in different families but have in common the unique ability to inflate themselves (with water if they are in water or air if they are out of water) into a ball. This is a protective device making them larger in size and therefore more difficult to swallow when they are attacked. The porcupinefishes have the additional protection of spines all over their body with which to deter enemies. When the fish are inflated these spines stick out like a pincushion, making them a very unpalatable morsel indeed.

Puffers, especially members of the genus *Canthigaster*, are often kept by marine aquarists. They are fairly hardy, colorful, and not difficult to feed. Although bite-sized bits of food are preferred, they have the ability to nibble pieces off larger chunks of things like shrimp, fish, and clams that were probably placed in the tank for larger fishes.

Porcupinefishes are very attractive as juveniles and often appear very comical, providing many hours of pleasant aquarium watching for the aquarist. They do grow large, so allowance for this growth must be taken into account when the size of the aquarium is determined.

BUTTERFLYFISHES

Butterflyfishes are favorites of marine aquarists, and at least one butterflyfish is kept at one time or another in every marine tank. Unfortunately, they are not the easiest of fishes to keep, and many who have tried them have failed. There are successes, however, and even verified cases where butterflyfishes have been kept in excess of six to seven years. These delicate creatures have virtually no means of defense other than their dorsal spines and ability to flee quickly from danger.

The problems with butterflyfishes in aquaria are basically threefold: (1) they are difficult to feed; (2) other fishes bother them by chasing them, nipping their fins, or preventing them from getting at the food; and (3) they are quick to fall victim to diseases. Once these problems are overcome the butterflyfishes will continue to live and delight the aquarist for many years. Butterflyfishes will take brine shrimp (living at first but eventually frozen) and other small bits of food of similar type but should receive some vegetable matter as well for a more balanced diet. Vitamin supplements should be added. If the butterflyfish refuses food, place some on one of the coral decorations as described earlier in an attempt to get them started.

Most of the butterflyfishes are roughly similar in shape (though quite different in color pattern) and easily recognizable as butterflyfishes. Among the favorites in marine aquaria are a few species that depart from the "normal" shape by having an extended snout. These long-nosed butterflyfishes (*Forcipiger* spp.) can probe among the coral decorations with their long snouts and reach bits of food that others in the tank cannot. They are generally a bit hardier than the bulk of the other butterflyfish species.

ANGELFISHES

One of the most colorful groups of fishes kept in marine aquaria is the angelfishes. From the smaller species of the genus *Centropyge* to the large *Pomacanthus* and *Holacanthus* species, almost every one is adorned with bright colors. In addition, most of them (excluding *Centropyge*) change their patterns and colors drastically as they grow from juvenile to adult. Very familiar to aquarists are the *Pomacanthus* species that as juveniles sport a velvety black background color crossed by stripes, arcs, or even circles of white or yellow.

1

2

3

4

Centropyge bispinosus.
2. *Zanclus canescens*
juvenile. 3. *Zanclus
canescens*, the Moorish
idol. 4. *Paracanthurus
hepatus*. 5. *Acanthurus
eucosternon*, the powder
ue tang. (Photos 1, 4 & 5.
.l. 2. Dr. D. Terver, Nancy
Aquarium. 3. K.H. Choo.)

5

Angelfishes are very unsociable when it comes to members of their own species. Normally when two small angelfishes, for instance the French or gray angelfishes of the Caribbean, are placed in the same aquarium it is not long before they are scrapping with resultant ragged fins. It is therefore strongly recommended that two such angelfishes not be kept in the same tank unless it is so large that their encounters are few and far between (although they often seem to be able to find each other and start feuding).

Angelfishes in nature eat a wide variety of organisms from coral polyps and sponges to small crustaceans as well as vegetable matter in the form of algae. In the aquarium their diet should also be as varied as possible and include vegetable matter as well. Young angelfishes in nature are often parasite pickers, a behavior that they sometimes exhibit in aquaria, much to the delight of the aquarist who welcomes a means of ridding his tank of unwanted parasites.

SURGEONFISHES and MOORISH IDOLS

The bright colors of the surgeonfishes have attracted the attention of marine aquarists, and these fishes are often kept in a marine community tank. They are not antisocial like the damsels or angelfishes and can usually be kept safely with most other fishes including butterflyfishes. Although their main means of defense is flight like the butterflyfishes, they do have a sharp anteriorly-directed spine on each side of their caudal peduncle which can inflict quite a bit of damage to other fishes and the aquarist as well. They should be handled with care when netted to prevent accidents.

Surgeonfishes are mostly herbivores grazing on the algae and plants of the reefs or adjacent areas in large schools. It is therefore mandatory that they be given vegetable matter in their diets, although this can be supplemented to some extent with animal flesh such as brine shrimp, clams, shrimp, and fish.

Surgeonfishes (or tangs as they are sometimes called) are not small fishes as adults, reaching lengths of up to a foot in some cases, and should be housed in relatively large tanks. They are good community fishes and their colors, especially those species such as the powder blue tang *(Acanthurus leucosternon)* and blue surgeonfish *(Paracanthurus hepatus)*, do much to brighten up any marine tank.

The combination of form and color of the Moorish idol *(Zanclus canescens)* has made this one of the most prized of aquarium fishes. The long, flowing dorsal fin filament and the black, yellow and white pattern have attracted so much attention that this fish is often used as the basis for a pattern or design. It is difficult to walk through a department store without spotting something which bears a Moorish idol motif.

Unfortunately, this is one of the most difficult fishes to keep. Moorish idols are quite reluctant to start feeding in the aquarium or, if they do, they seem to miss something in their diet which apparently is essential to their well-being. Some aquarists succeeded in keeping them for an extended period, but most are apparently doomed to failure. One thing is known to be essential, and that is a very large tank. Their shape also dictates that the tank be deep. They seem to be very delicate, and the long, flowing dorsal fin filament attracts the attention of other tankmates which constantly nip at it. This constant irritation, not to mention the physical damage, usually contributes much to their early demise. Since their price remains relatively high (they do not ship well and many die before they ever reach their destinations), these difficult fish are not recommended except for the advanced marine hobbyist who has at least a fighting chance to keep them for a reasonable length of time.

1. *Pseudochromis paccagnellae.* 2. *Pseudochromis porphyreus.* 3. *Gramma loreto* (note the pattern similar to above). 4. *Anthias pleurotaenia.* 5. *Cromileptes altivelis.* (Photos 1. Allan Power. 2. Roger Lubbock. 3. CLI. 4. Aaron Norman. 5. H. Hansen.)

GROUPERS AND THEIR RELATIVES

The groupers and grouper-like fishes are usually very hardy and easily maintained. They are known for their large mouths and correspondingly large appetites. Small chunks of fish, shrimp, squid, clams, etc. are avidly taken as well as any fish placed in the tank that is small enough. The aquarist must therefore choose their tankmates carefully by size to make sure this does not happen. Groupers are also prone to hiding among the coral decorations in holes or caves where they keep an eye on the goings-on in the tank, watching for something that they can eat to come into range. A quick dash from their "lair" usually ends in the disappearance of some tidbit (or fish), after which they return from whence they came just as quickly.

Most groupers are very large fishes, so only the juveniles are kept. Since they outgrow their tank very quickly, they do not have the popularity of many of the other fishes with more color that remain smaller and therefore can be kept for a longer time. A few, such as the blue-and-yellow reef grouper (*Epinephelus flavocaeruleus*), are maintained when they are available. The larger groupers do have one big redeeming character—they can become very tame even to the point of being "petted" and fed by hand.

The polkadot or leopard grouper *(Cromileptes altivelis)* and the golden striped grouper *(Grammistes sexlineatus)* are other species that have found favor in marine tanks, along with the comet *(Calloplesiops altivelis).* They are not as easy to maintain as some of the *Epinephelus* species, but are not very difficult either. A little extra care is all that is needed to ensure their longevity in a tank.

Anthiids are grouper relatives that are starting to appear for sale more and more. It was not too long ago that the lyretail coralfish *(Anthias squamipinnis)* was the only one of this group available on a regular basis. Then came the very popular purple queen *(Mirolabrichthys tuka)*, and now at least a half dozen others can be obtained. They are mostly plankton or small animal feeders and survive very well on a diet of brine shrimp supplemented by a variety of other prepared or live foods.

Among the smaller grouper-like fishes for marine aquaria are the grammas *(Gramma)* and the dottybacks *(Pseudochromis)*. The royal gramma from the Caribbean *(Gramma loreto)* is the best known and may even be one of the "standard" fishes for a marine tank. Its striking magenta and yellow colors are hard to pass by when selecting the fishes for a tank. Royal grammas tend to be shy and do not get along well with members of their own kind. They are not as hardy as many of the other groupers and are sensitive to acid water. As long as proper conditions are maintained, however, the fish will not only survive but there is a chance that actual spawning may take place. It is interesting to note that one of the dottybacks *(Pseudochromis paccagnellae)* from the Western Pacific has a similar magenta and yellow color pattern. Other dottybacks are just as brilliantly colored (two are solid magenta) and should be cared for in the same manner as the grammas, although they are a bit more sociable.

BATFISHES

Among the marine fishes recommended for beginners is the orbiculate batfish *(Platax orbicularis)*. It is hardy, feeds well on a variety of foods, grows amazingly fast, and is interesting in its habits. Its color and shape are such that it is a nearly perfect replica of a dead leaf. To enhance this appearance the batfish will swim on its side among such leaves and be almost indistinguishable from them. Orbiculate batfish are easily tamed and will shortly be taking food directly from their owner's hand. They are heavy feeders and put on weight and size at a very fast rate. It is only a short time before a 2"-3" tall batfish becomes a 12"-14" batfish. Large tanks are therefore a must when keeping these fish.

1
2
3

4

1. *Lienardella fasciata*, one of the Pacific wrasses. 2. *Anampses twistii,* with its pair of ocellated spots. 3. *Zebrasoma flavescens*, delicate but beautiful. 4. *Labroides dimidiatus* (the cleaner wrasse) and *Thalassoma lutescens* juvenile. (Photos 1. Michio Goto. 2. Helmut Debelius. 3. Dr. Gerald R. Allen. 4. CLI.)

Much more beautiful but also much more delicate is the pinnatus batfish *(Platax pinnatus)*. Those who were able to keep the orbiculate batfish so easily and thought the pinnatus would be just as easy were in for a rude shock. They seem to be more reluctant to start feeding and are more prone to disease than their cousin. This fish is therefore not recommended for the beginner but only for the more advanced hobbyist. The pinnatus also mimics dead leaves, but those blackened leaves with light edges that coincide with the black body color and orange trim of the fish. It grows to a similarly large size as the orbiculate batfish, and a large tank is recommended.

WRASSES

The wrasses (family Labridae) are a very diverse group of fishes with almost as diverse needs. Many are commonly kept in marine aquaria with mixed results. Cleaner wrasses of the genus *Labroides*, for instance, are difficult to keep alive mainly, it seems, because of their specific feeding habits. They are full-time parasite pickers and usually will not take to any of the foods offered to marine aquarium fishes. Once the parasites are gone from the fishes in the tank the cleaners slowly starve to death.

Many wrasses are sand divers. They will, at night or when frightened, bury themselves in the sand. This causes many problems when the aquarist wants to remove them from the aquarium. As soon as the wrasse is chased it disappears into the sand. The aquarist must then run his fingers (or some other object that will not hurt the fish) through the sand until his quarry pops up. The net is readied again and the chase continues until the wrasse dives back into the sand. The tank usually looks like a mess by the time the fish is netted. Young *Coris* exhibit this type behavior. For this reason tanks with wrasses should have a sufficient amount of sand or gravel on the bottom.

Juvenile wrasses look quite different from the adults, and

adult females often look quite different from the adult males. This is one of the families in which there are "supermales," males that have a completely different color pattern than the normal males and females (which look alike) of the same species. The normal males and females will spawn together in a school with the eggs and sperm released simultaneously as the fishes swirl around. Some males, (the supermales) however, grow a bit larger and develop completely different color patterns. These males spawn with the normally colored females but on an individual basis, not along with the school.

Wrasses are generally not too difficult to keep and will survive on many of the standard marine aquarium foods. They can be kept in community tanks as long as the other fishes are active enough to get their share of the food, for the wrasses are quick and often clean up everything before such fishes as butterflyfishes can even get started. Since the wrasses are so diverse and no general account can cover the wide variation in habits and food preferences, it is best to check with the shopkeeper about the individual species.

CARDINALFISHES

Although a number of cardinalfishes are available, only a few species have ever gained any amount of popularity in the marine aquarium. One of the reasons for this is that most cardinalfishes are nocturnal, hiding during the day and only becoming active at twilight or at night. This causes problems with feeding since they will be hiding during the normal feeding hours and must be specially fed in the evenings. They do not grow very large but do take to aquarium foods quickly. As long as they have some dark or subdued light area in which to spend the daylight hours, they will do fairly well.

Perhaps the most popular of the cardinalfishes is the pajama cardinal *(Sphaeramia nematoptera)*. Its black bar and red-spotted pattern is quite different from that of most

1

2

4

1. *Cephalopholis argus*. 2. *Amphiprion clarkii*. 3. *Aluterus scriptus*. 4. *Zanclus canescens*. 5. *Arothron mappa*. 6. *Fistularia petimba*. 7. *Lutjanus sebae*. 8. *Lutjanus kasmira*. 9. *Priacanthus cruentatus*. 10. *Naso brevirostris*. (Photos 1-3, 5-8. M. Goto, 4. Dr. D. Terver).

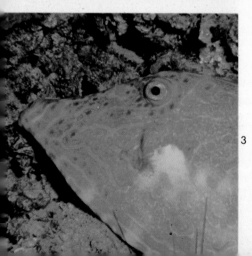

3

5

8

6

9

7

10

other cardinalfishes, and a small school of them is a most pleasing sight in an aquarium. They are most active in the evenings and as easily fed as the other cardinalfishes. It has been reported that the pajama cardinalfish is a mouth-brooder.

GOBIES

Gobies are among the most aptly suited fishes for life in an aquarium. They are generally small, only a few inches long, hardy, colorful, inexpensive, and stand a good chance of being spawned. Yet for some obscure reason they are bypassed, except for a few species that have, because of the above attributes, become popular. Number one among these is undoubtedly the neon goby *(Gobiosoma oceanops)* from the Caribbean. These small gobies, not more than 2"-3" long, have graced marine aquaria for many years. They will do well on live brine shrimp plus a variety of other foods and will pick parasites from the other inhabitants of the aquarium if any appear. To add to their desirability, there have been many instances where they have spawned, although very few have been raised even to the free-swimming stages.

A second very popular goby, but one that has all but disappeared from the hobby because of conservation laws, is the Catalina goby *(Lythrypnus dalli)*. It rivals the neon in color with its orange body and neon blue stripes, but its disposition leaves much to be desired. Only one Catalina goby can be placed in a tank, otherwise fights will break out. In both the Catalina goby and neon goby the colors are greatly enhanced by the use of special fluorescent lights.

EELS

Very few eels are kept in marine aquaria. This is partly due to their size and partly due to the fact that the more colorful ones, the morays, are dangerous. They have sharp teeth that can inflict a nasty wound if a finger gets in their way in the aquarium or when they are netted. Small morays are often available and do well in home aquaria. They seek out a hiding place where they spend most of their time with their head sticking out. Feeding morays is difficult, although once they are started they usually cause no further problem. Squid is a delicacy to the morays and should be tried with the more reluctant feeders. Normally a squid dropped in front of a moray will not be touched at first. With luck it will be taken after a while. For the more daring aquarist the squid can be dangled in front of the nose of the moray, the motion usually enticing it to strike. But this can be dangerous if the eel misjudges the distance and hits the fingers instead.

The only other eels commonly kept are the ribbon eels *(Rhinomuraena)*. Only one or two species are known and are kept because of the color (bright blue or black with yellow) and the unusual nasal fringes that give them their scientific name. Their care and feeding are similar to that for the morays. They are more adept than moray eels, however, in getting out of the tank through a small opening, so constant checks must be made to be sure that they are still "at home."

DRAGONETS

Dragonets (members of the family Callionymidae) were almost unheard of in marine aquaria until recent years, when two species, *Synchiropus splendidus* and *S. picturatus,* came upon the scene. Their bright colors and patterns made them instant hits. Unfortunately they are quarrelsome, and the recommendation is that only one be kept in a tank. Feeding is not difficult, although it is necessary to see that the food does get down through the water column to the bottom where they spend their time. They generally remain hidden much of the time but once in a while will scoot across the tank from one point of refuge to another.

1. *Zanclus canescens.* 2. *Pterois volitans.* 3. *Cantherhines dumerilii.* 4. *Gaterin orientalis.* 5. *Platax pinnatus.* 6. *Upeneus tragula.* 7. *Scorpaenopsis cirrhosa.* 8. *Scolopsis bimaculatus.* 9. *Carcharhinus* sp. 10.*Diodon hystrix.* 11. *Thalassoma lunare.* (All M. Goto photos).

GOATFISHES

Goatfishes are also bottom fishes and must be fed in a way that their food is not intercepted by other hungry fishes on the way down. They become excited when food is placed in the tank and swim along the bottom with their barbels moving about rapidly. These barbels are sensory, and when they touch a bit of food it is quickly engulfed. Goatfishes may cause a problem for aquarists who prefer to keep a layer of fine sand on the bottom. As they move back and forth in the tank with the barbels searching for food, the fine sand is stirred up causing the tank to almost always look "foggy." At night the goatfishes are usually quiescent and, as they sleep, change to a more blotchy pattern.

SQUIRRELFISHES

Squirrelfishes, like the cardinalfishes, are nocturnal. When most of the other fishes have quieted down for the night the squirrelfishes begin their search for food. If it is not available at the correct time they will usually go hungry—at least until their hunger becomes greater than their fear of coming out in the bright light and they quickly dart out for a morsel or two of food. Because of this dislike for light areas, squirrelfishes should be provided with places to hide during the day or when the aquarium light is on. Since they are predators, they are not difficult to feed and it is wise not to place in their tank any fishes small enough for them to swallow. Almost all of the squirrelfishes are red in color, with varying patterns of white stripes or lines. They can be kept in small groups without harm.

SNAPPERS AND THEIR RELATIVES

Juvenile snappers are commonly kept in home aquaria, but most species eventually grow too big and must be given or traded away to someone with a larger tank. A few species have gained some measure of popularity—the blue-striped snapper *(Lutjanus kasmira),* the blood-red snapper *(L.*

erythropterus), and the red emperor *(L. sebae)* being the most commonly seen. They are hardy fishes and easily kept, but are predatory and cannot be kept with fishes small enough for them to swallow.

Close relatives of the snappers are the sweetlips of the family Gaterinidae. Juveniles of several species are kept but, like the snappers, are too large as adults, attaining lengths in some species of up to three feet. The most popular of the sweetlips are the clown sweetlips *(Gaterin chaetodonoides)* and the oriental sweetlips *(Gaterin orientalis)*, both very attractive as juveniles but more sedately colored as adults. They are good community fishes but are apt to be a bit shy and retiring, requiring sufficient hiding places during the day. They will accept a wide variety of foods, but their mouths are not as large as that of the snappers and the pieces should be correspondingly smaller.

Other relatives of the snappers include fishes such as scolopsids, nemipterids, pentapodids, and grunts which occasionally turn up in aquarium stores. They can generally be handled in much the same manner as the snappers and gaterins.

HAWKFISHES
Hawkfishes are small scorpionfish-like fishes that are often seen perched on coral heads waiting for some small prey animal to pass by. If danger threatens they move down among the coral branches where they are relatively safe. They exhibit this same behavior in the aquarium. Only a few species are ever seen, the most interesting and popular of which is the long-nosed hawkfish *(Oxycirrhites typus)*. Live brine shrimp are the recommended food but other types of marine aquarium fare are accepted. Small guppies are quickly dispatched.

1. *Platax orbicularis*. 2. *Parupeneus spilurus*. 3. *Amphiprion perideraion*. 4. *Aulostomus chinensis*. 5. *Balistoides conspicillum*. 6. *Pomacanthus semicirculatus*. (Photos 2 - 6, M. Goto. 1, CLI.)

OTHER FISHES

A large number of other fishes are kept in marine aquaria, ranging from the flatfishes, which lie on the bottom doing their best to imitate the color and pattern of the gravel, to the frogfishes (*Antennarius* spp.), which "angle" for small fishes with their rod and lure. Also in the frogfish family is the sargassumfish *(Histrio histrio)*, which blends in quite well with its surroundings of sargassum seaweed as it snaps up unsuspecting small fishes, shrimps, crabs, and the like that also live there. The problem with these fishes is not to find food for them but trying to keep them from eating up everything in sight—including each other.

There are very few marine catfishes but one group, the plotosids, are kept in aquaria as juveniles. They are prettily striped with yellow or white and spend their time scouring the bottom for bits of food with their sensory barbels. Care should be taken in handling plotosids since their dorsal and pectoral fin spines are capable of inflicting very painful wounds. Normal aquarium foods that will sink to the bottom are suitable.

Juvenile drums of the genera *Pareques* and *Equetus* are very popular because of the elongate anterior portion of the dorsal fin. The common names of two of the species refer to this characteristic—highhat and jackknife fish. Very small individuals tend to be somewhat delicate, but otherwise they are not difficult to maintain. Holes and caves should be provided for these shy fishes.

One of the most unusual fishes for the marine aquarium is the pinecone fish *(Monocentris japonicus)*. This little armored fish gets its common name from its pinecone-like appearance, formed by modified scales. In addition it has light organs near the tip of the lower jaw, the light being produced by commensal luminescent bacteria. Their natural food is small crustaceans, so they can easily be coaxed onto live brine shrimp.

For the advanced aquarist with exceptionally large tanks,

there are a few sharks that can be kept. Some of the smaller bottom species are nicely patterned and not difficult to keep. Crustaceans and fishes form the basis of their diet.

These are only some of the more common fishes or families that are available to marine aquarists. In almost every shipment from far off oceans there is something new to be seen—perhaps only a different species of an already well-known group, but occasionally something that causes the aquarist to dig out his reference books to find out what it is. This makes the marine aquarium hobby much more interesting and satisfying to those who have taken it up. The challenge is there but the rewards for accepting it are very great.

Young drums, like this *Equetus acuminatus* or high hat, tend to be delicate when small but are more hardy as they grow larger. Photo by G. Marcuse.